Learn Rebol

Practical Guide

A. De Quattro

Copyright © 2024

Guide to Rebol

1.Introduction to Rebol

Rebol is a programming language created by Carl Sassenrath in 1997. Characterized by a clean and simple design, Rebol was developed with the goal of being a versatile and easy-to-learn language. Its capabilities lie primarily in data processing and the creation of scripts for automating repetitive tasks.

One of Rebol's distinctive features is its concise and readable syntax, making it suitable for both beginners and experienced programmers. Rebol's approach is based on the concept of "dialects", which are small variations of the language that allow for writing code in a more intuitive and specific way for a particular function.

Rebol supports various programming paradigms, including procedural, functional, and object-oriented programming. Thanks to its flexibility, Rebol can be used for a wide range of applications, from creating simple scripts for automating common tasks to implementing complex systems and web applications.

In this introduction to Rebol, we will explore the main features of the language, its capabilities, and how to start using it to develop software. We will start with the basic syntax of Rebol, then move on to practical examples and algorithms to fully understand the potential of this language.

Features of Rebol

Rebol is a powerful and versatile programming language, with several features that set it apart from other languages. Here are some of the main features of Rebol:

- Concise syntax: Rebol's syntax is designed to be readable and understandable, with a concise notation that allows for writing code efficiently and directly.

- Dynamic typing: Rebol is a dynamically typed language, meaning that it is not necessary to explicitly declare the data type of a variable. This makes application development simpler and faster, as there is no need to worry about data types.

- Automatic memory management: Rebol automatically manages memory, freeing up memory allocated for unused variables and reducing the risk of memory leaks.

- Multitasking: Rebol supports multitasking through mechanisms such as threads and processes, allowing for the execution of multiple tasks simultaneously and fully utilizing system resources.

- Structured data: Rebol supports structured

data such as lists, arrays, and objects, making it easier to organize and manage data within an application.

- Networking support: Rebol offers built-in functionality for network communications, allowing for the creation of web applications and client/server applications with ease.

- User interface: Rebol includes a graphical toolkit for creating user interfaces, enabling the rapid development of applications with an intuitive and pleasant interface.

- Extensibility: Rebol is an extensible language, allowing for the definition of new functionalities and extensions through the use of plugins and modules.

Rebol Syntax

Rebol's syntax is characterized by a simple and direct notation, making it easy to write code and increase readability. Instructions in Rebol are generally written as sequences of keywords followed by parameters or arguments, without the need for punctuation or parentheses.

For example, to assign a value to a variable in Rebol, the following syntax is used:

```
variable_name: value
```

To perform a sum between two numbers:

```
sum: 3 + 4
```

To create a list of values:

```
list: [1 2 3 4 5]
```

Rebol uses the concept of blocks to define sequences of values or instructions. A block is delimited by square brackets, and can contain a list of values, instructions, or other data structures.

```
my_block: ["Hello, World!" 42 [1 "two" 3]]
```

Functions in Rebol are defined using the keyword `func`, followed by a list of arguments and the function body delimited by curly braces.

```
func sum [a b] [
    return a + b
]
```

Rebol also supports functional programming, allowing for the definition of anonymous functions and passing them as arguments to other functions.

```
double: func [x] [
    return x * 2
]
```

```
result: map [1 2 3 4] :double
```

Practical Examples

To better understand Rebol's capabilities, it is useful to explore some practical examples of code. Below, I will show an example of how to write a simple script in Rebol to calculate the sum of two numbers entered by the user.

```
print "Enter the first number: "
number1: to-integer ask ""

print "Enter the second number: "
number2: to-integer ask ""

sum: number1 + number2
```

```
print rejoin ["The sum of" number1 "and" number2 "is" sum]
```

In this script, the user is asked to enter two numbers, which are then summed and the result is displayed on the screen.

Another interesting example is the creation of a recursive function to calculate the factorial of a number in Rebol.

```
fact: func [n] [
    if n = 0 [return 1]
    return n * fact n - 1
]
```

```
print fact 5
```

In this example, the `fact` function calculates the factorial of a number `n` using recursion.

Conclusion

Rebol is a versatile and powerful programming language that offers a simple and intuitive syntax for software development. Its distinctive features, such as dynamic typing, automatic memory management, and support for multitasking, make it suitable for a wide range of applications and contexts.

With an active community and online resources available for learning and deepening knowledge of Rebol, it is possible to use this language to realize innovative projects and efficiently automate complex tasks.

In this brief introduction, we have seen the main features of Rebol, its syntax, and some practical examples to start programming with this language. With practice and experience, it is possible to develop advanced skills in Rebol and fully leverage its potential to create sophisticated and innovative applications.

2. Rebol Installation

Rebol is a dynamic programming language, known for its simplicity, flexibility, and ease of learning. In this guide, I will show you how to install and set up the Rebol development environment, so you can start creating your own applications and scripts quickly and effectively.

Before proceeding with the installation, it is important to ensure that you have an operating system compatible with Rebol. Currently, Rebol supports the Windows, MacOS, and Linux operating systems, so make sure you have one of these operating systems installed on your computer.

Once you have verified the operating system, you can proceed with the installation of Rebol. First, you need to download the installation package from the official Rebol website (https://www.rebol.com). Once the installation file is downloaded, you can start the installation process by double-clicking on the file icon.

During the installation, you will be asked to accept the license terms and select the installation directory. It is recommended to keep the default settings unless you want to specify a different installation directory. Once the installation is complete, Rebol will be ready to use.

After installing Rebol, you can start the development environment to begin creating your own scripts and applications. To do this, simply open the terminal or command prompt of your operating system and type the command to start the Rebol interpreter.

Once the Rebol interpreter is running, you can start writing your own code. Rebol is a very simple and readable language, based on a system of values and blocks. For example, the following Rebol code prints the phrase "Hello, World!" to the screen:

```rebol
print "Hello, World!"
```

The Rebol language offers many constructs and functions to help programmers create more complex and functional scripts. For example, you can define custom functions, create variables, handle user input, and more.

To assist programmers in developing with Rebol, there is also extensive official documentation available on the Rebol website. This documentation provides detailed information about all language features, as well as code examples and tutorials to help programmers learn and use Rebol effectively.

In addition to the basic interpreter, the Rebol development environment also includes additional tools to support programmers in developing and debugging their scripts and applications. For example, there is an integrated debugger that helps quickly and efficiently identify and correct errors in the code.

To configure the Rebol development environment optimally, you can customize settings and preferences according to your needs and preferences. For example, you can configure code formatting, configuration file management, and more.

Furthermore, Rebol also supports the use of external libraries and add-on modules to extend the language's capabilities and create more complex and advanced applications. These libraries can be easily imported into your code and used to add new features and capabilities to your applications.

The installation and configuration of the Rebol development environment is a simple and quick process, allowing programmers to start creating scripts and applications quickly and effectively. With its simplicity and flexibility, Rebol proves to be a great language for developing a wide range of applications and scripts that can run on different operating systems and architectures.

3. Syntax and coding rules in Rebol

Rebol is a programming language that stands out for its extreme flexibility and conciseness. This is mainly due to its minimalist syntax and its ability to handle a wide range of data types uniformly. When writing code in Rebol, it is important to follow some basic rules that allow for writing clean, readable, and well-structured code.

A fundamental aspect of Rebol syntax is that it does not require the use of parentheses to define expressions. Instead, expressions are delimited by spaces. For example, to define the sum of two numbers, you simply write:

```rebol
a: 10
b: 20
c: a + b
```

```

In this example, the variables `a` and `b` are initialized with the values 10 and 20 respectively, and the variable `c` is assigned with the sum of `a` and `b`. It is important to note that Rebol is a case-insensitive language, so it does not distinguish between upper and lower case letters.

Variables are declared within a code block using the symbol `:`. For example, to assign a value to a variable, you write:

```rebol
name: "Mario"
```

In this case, the variable `name` is initialized with the string "Mario". You can use variables of different data types in Rebol, such as
```

numbers, strings, dates, data blocks, and much more. Additionally, Rebol has a dynamic typing mechanism, which means it is not necessary to specify the type of a variable when it is declared.

To define a function in Rebol, you use the keyword `func`, followed by the function parameters enclosed in parentheses and separated by spaces. For example, to define a function that calculates the sum of two numbers, you write:

```rebol
sum: func [a b][
    return a + b
]
```

In this example, the function `sum` accepts two parameters `a` and `b` and returns their sum. To call the function and get the result, you simply write:

```rebol
result: sum 10 20
```

The value returned by the function is then stored in the variable `result`.

Rebol also provides a mechanism for handling exceptions using the `catch` and `throw` keywords. For example, to handle an exception that occurs within a code block, you use the following syntax:

```rebol
catch [
    ; code block that may generate an exception
```

```
    throw "Error!"
] [
    print "Handled error!"
]
```

In this example, the code block inside the square brackets is executed, and if an exception occurs, the string "Error!" is thrown. The `catch` keyword catches the exception and handles it in the following block of code.

It is important to note that Rebol also supports object-oriented programming (OOP) through the use of objects, methods, and classes. For example, to define a class in Rebol, you use the code block `{ }`:

```rebol
```

```
Point: make object! [
    x: 0
    y: 0
    move: func [dx dy][
        x: x + dx
        y: y + dy
    ]
]
```

In this example, a class `Point` is defined with two attributes `x` and `y` and a method `move` that moves the point by a certain amount along the x and y axes. To create an instance of the class and call the method, you use the following syntax:

```rebol
p: make Point []
```

```
p:move 10 20
```

The variable `p` is initialized as an instance of the `Point` class, and the `move` method is called with the parameters `10` and `20`.

In Rebol, you can also work with data blocks, which are very versatile and flexible data structures. Blocks are defined using square brackets `[ ]` and can contain values of different types. For example, to define a data block, you write:

```rebol
data: ["Mario" 30 true]
```

In this case, a data block is defined that contains a string, a number, and a boolean value. You can access elements of the block using the `at` access operator. For example, to access the first element of the block, you write:

```rebol
print data at 1
```

This code will print the string "Mario" to the screen.

Finally, Rebol allows you to define comments within the code using the symbol `;`. For example, to comment a line of code, you write:

```rebol
; This is a comment
```

Comments are ignored by the Rebol interpreter during code execution and serve to document how the program works to make it easier to understand.

Rebol is a very flexible and powerful programming language that allows for writing code in a concise and readable manner. Following the syntax and coding rules described above allows for creating well-structured and easy-to-maintain programs. With some practice and knowledge of these basic rules, you can fully leverage the capabilities of Rebol and create efficient and reliable applications.

4. Variables, data types, and basic operations in Rebol

In this chapter, we will delve into variables, data types, and basic operations in Rebol.

Variables:

In Rebol, variables are created by assigning them a value using the assignment operator ":=". For example:

```
variable: "value"
```

In this case, the variable takes on the value of the string type "value". Rebol is a dynamically typed language, which means you do not need to declare a variable's type before using it.

Data types:

Rebol supports various data types, including:

- Strings: sequences of characters enclosed in double quotes, for example "hello world".

- Numbers: integers or decimals, for example 42 or 3.14.

- Blocks: lists of values enclosed in square brackets, for example [1 2 3].

- Objects: complex data structures that group data and functions, similar to classes in other programming languages.

- Func: anonymous functions that can be assigned to variables and passed as arguments to other functions.

Basic operations:

In Rebol, you can perform a variety of basic operations on variables and data types, including:

- Assignment: as described earlier, you can assign a value to a variable using the assignment operator ":=".

- Concatenation: you can combine two or more strings using the concatenation operator "+". For example:

```
string1: "hello"

string2: " world"

result: string1 + string2
```

In this case, the value of "result" will be "hello world".

- Accessing elements of a block: you can access elements of a block using the index within square brackets. For example:

```
block: [1 2 3]

element: block[1]
```

In this case, the value of "element" will be 1.

- Function definition: you can define functions using the keyword "func". For example:

```
double: func [number][
    number * 2
]
result: double 5
```

In this case, the value of "result" will be 10.

- Flow control: Rebol supports flow control statements like "if", "else", and "loop" to conditionally or repetitively execute blocks of code.

- String manipulation: you can perform operations on strings such as searching for substrings, replacing characters, converting to uppercase/lowercase, and formatting.

- Block manipulation: Rebol offers a variety of built-in functions to work with blocks, including adding and removing elements, searching and replacing elements, concatenating and splitting blocks.

In conclusion, Rebol is a flexible and powerful programming language that provides a wide range of data types and basic operations for data manipulation and application development. Understanding variables, data types, and basic operations in Rebol is essential for writing efficient and functional code.

5. Conditions and conditional statements in Rebol

Conditional statements in Rebol allow you to execute a block of code only if a certain condition is met.

The most common conditional statements in Rebol are the following:

- IF: allows you to execute a block of code if a condition is met.

- EITHER: allows you to choose between two values based on a condition.

- SWITCH: allows you to execute different blocks of code based on the value of a variable.

- CASE: similar to SWITCH, but more flexible in handling different cases.

Below, we will describe in detail how to use these conditional statements in Rebol with practical examples.

1. IF:

The IF statement in Rebol allows you to execute a block of code if a certain condition is met. The syntax is as follows:

```rebol
if condition [
    ; code to execute if the condition is true
]
```

Example:

```rebol
```

```
num: 10
if num > 5 [
    print "The number is greater than 5"
]
```

In this example, the message "The number is greater than 5" will be printed on the screen because the condition `num > 5` is met.

2. EITHER:

The EITHER statement in Rebol allows you to choose between two values based on a certain condition. The syntax is as follows:

```rebol
either condition [
    true-value
```

```
][
    false-value
]
```

Example:

```rebol
status: true
result: either status [
    "Success"
][
    "Error"
]

print result
```

In this example, if the variable `status` is true, "Success" will be printed on the screen, otherwise "Error" will be printed.

3. SWITCH:

The SWITCH statement in Rebol allows you to execute different blocks of code based on the value of a variable. The syntax is as follows:

```rebol
switch value [
   case_1 [
      ; code for case 1
   ]
   case_2 [
      ; code for case 2
```

```
    ]
    default [
        ; code for cases not covered
    ]
]
```

Example:

```rebol
number: 2
switch number [
    1 [
        print "The number is one"
    ]
    2 [
        print "The number is two"
```

```
    ]
    default [
        print "The number is neither one nor two"
    ]
]
```

In this example, "The number is two" will be printed on the screen because the variable `number` has a value of 2.

4. CASE:

The CASE statement in Rebol is similar to SWITCH, but is more flexible in handling different cases. The syntax is as follows:

```rebol
```

```
case [
    condition_1 [
        ; code for case 1
    ]
    condition_2 [
        ; code for case 2
    ]
    default [
        ; code for cases not covered
    ]
]
```

Example:

```rebol
time: now/time
```

```
case [
    time < 12:00:00 [
        print "Good morning"
    ]
    time < 18:00:00 [
        print "Good afternoon"
    ]
    default [
        print "Good evening"
    ]
]
```

In this example, a different greeting will be printed on the screen based on the current time.

Conditional statements in Rebol allow you to

effectively manage the flow of the program based on different conditions. They are fundamental tools for writing code clearly and readably, making it easier to understand and maintain the software. I hope this guide has been helpful in understanding how to use conditional statements in Rebol.

6. Cycles and Iterations in Rebol

Rebol is a dynamic and functional programming language that provides a wide range of features to efficiently handle cycles and iterations. In this article, we will explore the concepts of cycles and iterations in Rebol and see some practical examples to better understand how to use them in code.

In Rebol, cycles and iterations are mainly handled through the control structure `loop`, which allows executing blocks of code repeatedly for a certain number of times or until a condition is met.

Defined Cycles

In Rebol, you can define cycles using the `loop` function following the syntax:

```
loop count [block]
```

Where `count` is the number of times the block of code will be executed and `block` is the code block to be executed. For example, if we want to print "Hello, world!" five times, we can write:

```
loop 5 [
    print "Hello, world!"
]
```

In this case, the code block `print "Hello, world!"` will be executed five times, printing "Hello, world!" each time.

Iterations with Index

In Rebol, you can use the iteration index within a cycle to keep track of the iterations and modify it during the cycle execution. The variable to keep track of the iteration index is usually named `i`, but it can be any other name chosen by the user.

```
loop 5 [
    print rejoin ["Iteration: " i]
    i: i + 1
]
```

In this example, we are printing the iteration index by adding 1 at each iteration. The result will be:

```
Iteration: 1
Iteration: 2
Iteration: 3
Iteration: 4
Iteration: 5
```

Conditional Cycles

In Rebol, you can create conditional cycles using the `while` function, which executes a block of code as long as a certain condition is met. The basic syntax of the `while` cycle is as follows:

```
while [condition] [
```

    block
]
```

For example, if we want to print even numbers up to 10, we can write:

```
i: 0

while [i <= 10] [

   if i mod 2 = 0 [

     print i

   ]

   i: i + 1

]
```
```

In this example, we increment the index `i` at each iteration and print only even numbers up to 10.

Iterating over Lists

In Rebol, you can iterate over a list of elements using the `foreach` function. The `foreach` function iterates over the elements of a list and applies a certain action to each element. The basic syntax of the `foreach` function is as follows:

```
foreach element [list] [
    block
]
```

For example, if we have a list of names and

we want to print them one per line, we can write:

```
names: ["Alice" "Bob" "Charlie" "David" "Eve"]
foreach name names [
    print name
]
```

In this example, we are printing each element of the `names` list one per line.

Nested Cycles

In Rebol, you can nest cycles, meaning to execute a cycle within another cycle. This is useful when you want to iterate over a complex data structure, such as a multidimensional array. For example, if we have a 2x2 matrix and we want to print all its elements, we can write:

```
matrix: [[1 2] [3 4]]
foreach row matrix [
    foreach item row [
        print item
    ]
]
```

In this example, we are iterating first over the rows of the matrix and then over the elements of each row.

Infinite Cycles

In Rebol, you can create infinite cycles using the `loop + forever` function. An infinite cycle is useful when you want to execute a block of code infinitely or until it is manually stopped by the user. For example, if we want to print a message infinitely, we can write:

```
loop [
    print "Hello, world!"
    wait 1  ; one-second pause
]
```

In this example, we are printing "Hello, world!" infinitely with a one-second pause between each print.

Practical Examples

Now that we have explored the concepts of cycles and iterations in Rebol, let's see some practical examples to illustrate how to use them in code.

Example 1: Sum Calculation

```
sum: 0
loop 10 [
    sum: sum + i
]
print sum
```

In this example, we are calculating the sum of the first 10 integers using a cycle. The result will be the sum of numbers from 1 to 10.

Example 2: Counting Vowels

```
vowels: 0
text: "Hello, world!"
foreach char text [
    switch/default char [
        "a" "e" "i" "o" "u" [
            vowels: vowels + 1
        ]
    ]
]
print vowels
```

In this example, we are counting the number of vowels present in a string using the `foreach` function and a switch-case to check if a character is a vowel.

Example 3: Printing a Pattern

```
pattern: "*"
loop 5 [
    print rejoin [copy pattern "**"]
]
```

In this example, we are printing a pyramid-shaped pattern using a cycle. The result will be:

```
*
***
```

```
*****
******
********
```

Conclusions

In this article, we have explored the concepts of cycles and iterations in Rebol, we have seen how to use the `loop` function to create cycles defining the number of iterations or exit conditions, how to use the iteration index to keep track of the number of iterations, and how to use the `foreach` function to iterate over lists of elements. We have also discussed conditional cycles, nested cycles, infinite cycles, and provided some practical examples to illustrate how to use cycles and iterations in Rebol. I hope this article has been helpful to you and has provided you with a broad insight into the programming techniques used to handle cycles and iterations in Rebol.

7. Definition and usage of Rebol functions

One of the most distinctive features of Rebol is the extensive use of functions as fundamental building blocks for programming. Functions in Rebol are extremely versatile and can be used in a variety of ways to manipulate data, create algorithms, and implement control logic.

Functions in Rebol are defined using the keyword "func" followed by a list of parameters in round parentheses and the instructions that make up the body of the function. Here is an example of how you can define a simple function in Rebol that returns the sum of two numbers:

```rebol
sum: func [a b] [
    a + b
```

]
```

In this example, the "sum" function takes two parameters, "a" and "b", and returns the sum of the two values. The function can be called by passing two numbers as arguments:

```rebol
>> print sum 2 3
5
```

Functions in Rebol can also be called without arguments, in which case you need to write empty round parentheses:

```rebol
>> print sum ()()

0
```

In addition to defining functions with parameters, Rebol supports anonymous functions, which can be stored in variables or passed as arguments to other functions. Here is an example of how you can define and use an anonymous function in Rebol:

```rebol
add-one: func [x] [
    x + 1
]

>> print add-one 5
6

>> map [1 2 3] func [x] [x * 2]

== [2 4 6]
```

Anonymous functions can be very useful when you want to pass custom code as an argument to a higher-order function, such as the "map" function in the second example above.

Functions in Rebol can also unconditionally return values using the keyword "return". Here is an example of how you can define a function that returns twice a number using "return":

```rebol
double: func [x] [
    return x * 2
]

```
>> print double 3
6
```

Functions in Rebol can also have optional parameters, which are defined using the "?" symbol after the parameter name in the parameter list. Here is an example of how you can define a function with an optional parameter in Rebol:

```rebol
greet: func [name ?greeting] [
    if not empty? greeting [
        return greeting name
    ]
    return "Hello, " name
]
```

```
>> print greet "Alice"

Hello, Alice


>> print greet "Bob" "Hi, "

Hi, Bob
```

In this example, the "greet" function takes a mandatory parameter, "name", and an optional parameter, "greeting". If the optional parameter is provided, the function will return the personalized greeting, otherwise it will return a default greeting.

Functions in Rebol can also be defined to accept a variable number of arguments, using the "..." symbol after the parameter name. Here is an example of how you can define a function that accepts a variable number of arguments and returns the sum of all values:

```rebol
multi-sum: func [...values] [
    total: 0
    foreach val values [
        total: total + val
    ]
    return total
]


>> print multi-sum 1 2 3
6
```

In this example, the "multi-sum" function accepts a variable number of arguments and uses a "foreach" loop to sum all the values passed to the function.

Functions in Rebol can also be defined as recursive functions, that is, functions that call themselves. Here is an example of how you can define a recursive function in Rebol that calculates the factorial of a number:

```rebol
factorial: func [n] [
    if n = 0 [
        return 1
    ]
    return n * factorial n - 1
]

>> print factorial 5
120
```

Recursive functions can be very useful for

solving problems that require the repetition of a certain process or algorithm.

In essence, functions are one of the key elements of programming in Rebol and provide developers with a powerful way to organize and reuse code efficiently. Functions in Rebol can be defined with a wide range of capabilities and can be used in many different ways to create complex and robust applications. Rebol functions are a fundamental tool for writing clean, modular, and easy-to-maintain code. With their flexibility and versatility, functions in Rebol offer developers an elegant way to address a wide range of programming problems effectively and efficiently.

8. Parameters and Returns of Rebol Functions

Rebol is a programming language known for its simplicity and flexibility. Among its most interesting features are functions, which allow you to define blocks of code that can be executed repeatedly.

When defining a function in Rebol, it is possible to specify input parameters that will be passed to the function when it is called. Parameters can be of different types, such as strings, numbers, code blocks, or even other functions. Additionally, you can specify return values that the function will provide once its execution is complete.

The syntax for defining a function in Rebol is as follows:

```rebol
```

```
function_name: func [parameter1 parameter2 ...] [

  code_blocks

  return return_value

]
```

where `function_name` is the name of the function you want to define, `parameter1`, `parameter2`, etc. are the parameters that will be passed to the function, `code_blocks` are the instructions the function should execute, and `return_value` is the value the function will return.

For example, suppose you want to define a simple function that adds two numbers passed as parameters and returns the result:

```rebol
```

```
sum: func [a b] [
  return a + b
]


print sum 3 5 ; prints 8
```

In the example above, the `sum` function takes two parameters `a` and `b`, adds the two numbers together, and returns the result.

You can also define functions without parameters by simply omitting the parameter list:

```rebol
greeting: func [
  print "Hello, world!"
]
```

```
greeting ; prints "Hello, world!"
```

If a function does not return any value, the `return` statement can be omitted.

Functions in Rebol can also be passed as arguments to other functions, just like any other data type. This allows for writing more modular and reusable code.

Example of passing a function as an argument:

```rebol
double: func [number] [
  return number * 2
]
```

```
apply_function: func [function argument] [
  return function argument
]

print apply_function :double 4 ; prints 8
```

In the above example, the `apply_function` function takes a function `function` and an argument `argument` as inputs, and returns the result of applying the function to the argument.

It is important to note that in Rebol, functions are considered first-class citizens, which means they can be assigned to variables, passed as arguments, and returned as values from other functions.

It is also possible to define anonymous functions, which are functions without a name and are defined directly within an expression. Anonymous functions are particularly useful when passing small functions as arguments to other functions.

Example of an anonymous function:

```rebol
apply_function: func [function argument] [
  return function argument
]

print apply_function func [number] [return number * 2] 4 ; prints 8
```

In the above example, an anonymous function that doubles a number is defined and passed as an argument to the `apply_function` function.

Lastly, it is important to highlight that in Rebol, recursive functions can be defined. These are functions that call themselves recursively until a base condition is met. This allows for implementing more complex algorithms efficiently and readably.

In conclusion, functions in Rebol are a powerful and flexible tool that allows for writing modular, reusable, and readable code. By leveraging Rebol's simple and intuitive syntax, functions with parameters and return values can be efficiently and effectively defined, making programming even more enjoyable and creative.

9. Handling and throwing exceptions in Rebol

Exception handling is a fundamental aspect of programming in any language, including Rebol. Exceptions are errors or unexpected situations that occur during the execution of the program and must be handled appropriately to ensure the proper execution of the code.

In Rebol, exceptions are handled using the TRY-CATCH-FINALLY code blocks. The TRY block contains the code that may generate an exception, while the CATCH block is executed if an exception occurs. The FINALLY block is always executed, regardless of whether an exception has occurred or not.

Here is an example of how to use TRY-CATCH-FINALLY in Rebol:

```
try [
    ; Here is where the code that may generate an exception is executed
    result: 10 / 0
] catch [
    ; Here the exception is handled
    print "Error during division by zero"
] finally [
    ; This block is always executed
    print "End of code execution"
]
```

In the example above, the TRY block contains a division by zero operation that will generate an exception. The CATCH block catches the exception and prints an error message, while the FINALLY block prints a message indicating the end of code execution.

In addition to the TRY-CATCH-FINALLY block, Rebol also provides the ability to manually throw exceptions using the RAISE function. This function can be used to report an error or abnormal situation during code execution.

Here is an example of how to throw an exception using the RAISE function:

```
if condition [
    raise make error! "Custom error"
]
```

In the example above, the IF statement checks

a condition and if the condition is true, an exception with a custom error message is thrown.

It is also possible to define custom exceptions in Rebol by creating new data types that represent specific errors. For example, you could create a data structure to handle invalid input errors:

```
invalid-input: make object! [
    message: "Invalid input"
    code: 1001
]


if invalid-input [
    raise make error! invalid-input
]
```

```

In the example above, a new data type make object! is created to represent an invalid input error. When an invalid input is detected, an exception is thrown using the created data structure.

In conclusion, exception handling is a crucial aspect of programming in Rebol and must be carefully addressed to ensure code robustness. By using TRY-CATCH-FINALLY blocks and the RAISE function, exceptions can be effectively managed to ensure that the code runs properly even in the presence of abnormal situations.
```

10. Debugging and testing of Rebol code

Debugging and testing code are two fundamental activities in software development, as they allow for the identification and correction of errors and issues in the source code. In this article, we focus on debugging and testing Rebol code, a functional and object-oriented programming language.

Debugging is the process of identifying and correcting errors in the source code. There are various tools and techniques that can be used for debugging Rebol code. One of the main tools is the debugger integrated into the language itself, which allows for step-by-step code execution and monitoring of variable states during execution.

Another useful tool for debugging Rebol code is printing variable values and executed instructions to the screen, which can be used to identify logic errors in the code. Additionally, logging statements can be used to log debug messages to log files and analyze any errors later on.

In Rebol code debugging, it is important to also pay attention to syntax and semantic errors, which can cause program malfunctions. Using tools such as text editors and compilers can help in identifying these types of errors.

An example of debugging Rebol code could be as follows:

```rebol
foreach item [1 2 3 4 5] [
    if item = 3 [
        print "Item found: 3"
    ]
```

]
```

In this example, the code searches for the element "3" in the list and prints a message if it finds it. However, if an error were to occur during code execution, such as a syntax error or a logic error, the debugger or printing variable values would need to be used to identify and correct the error.

Moving on to testing Rebol code, it is crucial to verify that the code works correctly and meets specific requirements. There are various testing techniques that can be used to test Rebol code, including manual testing and automated testing.

Manual testing involves running the code by a human being who manually checks if the code works correctly and produces the expected results. This technique is often used during
```

software development to verify the proper functioning of individual features.

On the other hand, automated testing involves implementing automated tests that are executed automatically to verify the correct operation of the software. One of the main tools used for automated testing of Rebol code is the testing module integrated into the language itself, which allows for easy and effective creation and execution of unit tests.

An example of a unit test in Rebol could be as follows:

```rebol
test: function [value] [
    if value > 0 [return true] [return false]
]
```

assert test 5

assert test 0

```

In this example, the test checks if the value passed as an argument to the function is greater than zero and returns true if the condition is true, otherwise it returns false. The two asserts verify if the expected results are correct and provide feedback in case of errors.

Testing Rebol code is important to ensure that the software is robust and error-free, and can be used in combination with debugging to identify and correct any issues in the source code. Furthermore, testing allows for verifying that the code meets specific requirements and that the features are implemented correctly.

Debugging and testing code are fundamental
```

activities in software development and are essential to ensure the quality and correctness of the software. By using appropriate tools and techniques, it is possible to identify and correct errors in Rebol code and verify that the software works correctly and meets specific requirements.

11. Creating User Interfaces with Rebol/View

Rebol/View is a programming language that allows you to easily create user interfaces for your applications. With Rebol/View, you can create windows, buttons, text boxes, and many other graphical elements in a simple and fast way. In this article, we will explain how to create user interfaces with Rebol/View, providing also some practical examples.

To start using Rebol/View, you first need to install the language on your system. Rebol/View is available for various platforms, including Windows, MacOS and Linux. Once Rebol/View is installed on your system, you can start creating user interfaces with the language.

To create a new window with Rebol/View, you can use the following syntax:

```rebol
view layout [box "Hello, world!"]
```

This code creates a simple window with a text box displaying the message "Hello, world!". It's important to note that Rebol/View code is based on code blocks, which are sequences of elements enclosed in square brackets.

In addition to simple text boxes, you can add other graphical elements to user interfaces created with Rebol/View. For example, you can add buttons, text boxes, dropdown menus, and many other graphical elements.

Here is a more complex example of how to create a user interface with various graphical elements using Rebol/View:

```rebol
view layout [
    hgroup [
        button "Open file" [print "You clicked the button"]
        field
        check "Option 1"
        check "Option 2"
        radio "Choice 1"
        radio "Choice 2"
    ]
    vgroup [
        text "This is a text"
        area "This is a text area"
    ]
]
```

In this example, we used the `hgroup` block to horizontally align the "Open file" button, text box, checkboxes, and radio buttons. We also used the `vgroup` block to vertically align the text and text area.

Rebol/View also allows you to handle events such as button clicks and text box changes. For example, you can use the following code to handle a button click event:

```rebol
view layout [
    button "Click here" [
        alert "You clicked the button!"
    ]
]
```

In this example, when you click the "Click here" button, an alert message will appear informing the user that they clicked the button.

Rebol/View also offers the possibility to use styles to customize the appearance of graphical elements. You can use predefined styles or create custom styles to adapt the user interface to your needs.

Here is an example of using a predefined style to change the color and size of a button:

```rebol
view layout [
    button "Click here" [
        alert "You clicked the button!"
    ]
    button "Another button" (style button
```

```
180x60 blue orange)
]
```

In this example, the first button uses the default style, while the second button uses a custom style that changes the button's color to blue and orange and increases its size to 180x60 pixels.

In conclusion, Rebol/View is a powerful programming language that allows you to create user interfaces for your applications in a simple and fast way. With Rebol/View, you can create windows, buttons, text boxes, and many other graphical elements, handle events such as button clicks and text box changes, and use styles to customize the appearance of graphical elements. We hope this article has provided you with the basics to start creating user interfaces with Rebol/View.

12. Management of events and interactions in Rebol

Managing events and interactions in Rebol is a fundamental aspect for creating interactive and dynamic applications. Rebol offers a very flexible event management system that allows developers to capture, filter, and respond to different types of events, such as mouse clicks, key presses, and touch interactions.

To handle events in Rebol, you can use the `do-events` function that allows the program to execute code when certain events occur. For example, the following code shows how to handle a `button-click` event:

```rebol
view layout [
    button "Click Me" [
        do-events [
```

```
        print "Button clicked!"
      ]
    ]
]
```

In this example, the `do-events` function is executed when the user clicks the button. Events can be filtered based on the type of event or other criteria using the `event` function along with a block of code. For example, we can capture only the `enter` key press events:

```rebol
view layout [
    field [
        do-events [
            if event/type = 'key and event/key = 'enter [
```

```
            print "Enter key pressed!"
        ]
      ]
    ]
]
```

In this case, the message is only printed when the user presses the `enter` key while the cursor is positioned in the input field.

Rebol also offers the ability to create complex interactions between different elements of the graphical interface. For example, we can create a "memory game" using the `do-events` function to handle click events on buttons:

```rebol
view layout [
```

style button-style button 50x50 effect [draw [pen black fill-pen white box 0x0 50x50]]

button-style "1" [

   do-events [

     face/text: pick ["X" "1"] face/effect/draw/color

     show face wait 1

   ]

]

button-style "2" [

   do-events [

     face/text: pick ["X" "2"] face/effect/draw/color

     show face wait 1

   ]

]

button-style "3" [

   do-events [

```
        face/text: pick [ "X" "3"]
face/effect/draw/color

        show face wait 1

    ]

  ]

]
```

In this example, we have three buttons with the text "1", "2", and "3". When the user clicks a button, the text temporarily changes to "X" to simulate the memory game.

Rebol also allows handling events not only in the graphical interface but also interacting with external systems like databases, web services, and third-party applications. For example, we can create an application that syncs with a remote database to display real-time information:

```rebol
data: load http://www.example.com/data.json

view layout [
    text-list data [
        do-events [
            print face/text
        ]
    ]
]
```

In this example, we load data from a remote JSON file and display the data in a text list. When the user selects an item from the list, the text of the selected item is printed.

The management of events and interactions in Rebol is a powerful aspect that allows developers to create interactive and dynamic applications. By using the `do-events` function, it's possible to capture, filter, and respond to different types of events, enabling the creation of intuitive and engaging user experiences. With examples like the "memory game" and interaction with remote databases, Rebol demonstrates its versatility and potential in developing sophisticated and high-performance applications.

13. File and Directory Manipulation with Rebol

Rebol is a programming language designed for manipulating data in a simple and efficient way. One of its main features is the ease with which you can manipulate files and directories thanks to its intuitive and versatile syntax.

To manipulate files and directories in Rebol, you can use the native functions provided by the language or create custom functions to adapt the language to your specific needs.

To create a new file in Rebol, you can use the `write` function, which allows you to write text to a specific file. For example, to create a new file named "test.txt" with the text "Hello, World!", you can use the following code:

```
```

```
write %test.txt "Hello, World!"
```

To read the contents of an existing file, you can use the `read` function, which returns the content of the file as a string. For example, to read the content of the previously created "test.txt" file, you can use the following code:

```
file-content: read %test.txt
print file-content
```

To copy a file from one directory to another, you can use the `copy-file` function, which copies the content of one file to another file. For example, to copy the "test.txt" file to the "backup" directory, you can use the following code:

```
copy-file %test.txt %backup/test.txt
```

To delete a file, you can use the `delete` function, which deletes the specified file from the system. For example, to delete the "test.txt" file, you can use the following code:

```
delete %test.txt
```

To create a new directory, you can use the `make-dir` function, which creates a new directory in the specified path. For example, to create a new directory named "backup", you can use the following code:

```
make-dir %backup
```

To delete a directory, you can use the `delete-dir` function, which deletes the specified directory from the system. It is important to note that the directory must be empty at the time of deletion. For example, to delete the previously created "backup" directory, you can use the following code:

```
delete-dir %backup
```

To list the contents of a directory, you can use the `list-dir` function, which returns a list of files and directories present in the specified path. For example, to list the contents of the current directory, you can use the following code:

```
dir-content: list-dir %.
print dir-content
```

To rename a file or directory, you can use the `rename` function, which renames the specified file or directory with the new name. For example, to rename the "test.txt" file to "hello.txt", you can use the following code:

```
rename %test.txt %hello.txt
```

These are just some examples of basic operations that can be performed to manipulate files and directories in Rebol. The language offers many other functions and options to adapt to the specific needs of each project. With its intuitive syntax and flexibility, Rebol is a powerful tool for managing files and directories quickly and efficiently.

14. Communicating with servers and external APIs in Rebol

One of the most useful features of Rebol is its ability to communicate with servers and external APIs in a simple and efficient way.

Communicating with a server or an external API means sending requests and receiving responses from a remote server. This is a common task for many modern applications, which often need to interact with web services to retrieve data or perform specific operations. In Rebol, this process is made very simple thanks to the presence of built-in functions that allow you to send and receive data through HTTP and other communication protocols.

To communicate with an external server in Rebol, you need to use the `read` or `write` function to send or receive data over a network connection. For example, to send a

GET request to a remote server and get the response data, you can use the following code:

```
response: read http://api.example.com/data
print response
```

In this example, the `read` function is used to send an HTTP GET request to the server at the address `http://api.example.com/data` and receive the response data. The received data is then stored in the variable `response` and printed to the screen using the `print` function.

You can also send POST or PUT requests using the `write` function. For example, to send a POST request with JSON data to a remote server and get the response data, you can use the following code:

```
data: make object! [key: "value"]

response: write http://api.example.com/update data

print response
```

In this case, an object `data` is created containing the data to send to the remote server. The `write` function is then used to send an HTTP POST request with the JSON data to the address `http://api.example.com/update` and receive the response data. The received data is stored in the variable `response` and printed to the screen.

Rebol also supports using external APIs through the `call` function. This function allows you to invoke an external API and get the response data directly in the desired format. For example, to get data from a

RESTful API and store it in a variable, you can use the following code:

```
response: call http://api.example.com/data
print response
```

In this case, the `call` function is used to invoke a RESTful API at the address `http://api.example.com/data` and get the response data directly in the desired format. The received data is then stored in the variable `response` and printed to the screen using the `print` function.

It is important to note that Rebol also supports using custom headers and authentication to communicate with servers and external APIs. For example, to send a request with a custom header and an authentication token, you can use the following code:

```
headers: make object! [
    Content-Type: "application/json"
    Authorization: "Bearer token"
]
response: read/custom http://api.example.com/data headers
print response
```

In this example, an object `headers` is created containing the Content-Type header and the Authorization header with the authentication token. The `read/custom` function is then used to send a request with the custom headers to the address `http://api.example.com/data` and receive the response data. The received data is then stored in the variable `response` and printed to the screen.

Communicating with servers and external APIs in Rebol is a simple and flexible process thanks to the built-in functions that allow you to send and receive data through HTTP and other communication protocols. By using the `read`, `write`, and `call` functions, you can send requests and get responses from servers and external APIs efficiently and intuitively. With the ability to use custom headers and authentication, you can also customize requests and ensure the security of the data exchanged with servers and external APIs.

15. Example of Application in Rebol

Software projects and development are processes that involve designing, developing, testing, and deploying software to solve problems and meet user needs. Software can be created for different platforms such as desktop, web, mobile, and embedded, and can be written in various programming languages such as Java, Python, C++, JavaScript, and many others.

One of the lesser-known but powerful programming languages is Rebol (Relative Expression Based Object Language), a scripting language that offers a simple yet powerful approach to writing code. Rebol was developed by Carl Sassenrath and offers many advanced features such as data manipulation, GUI creation, and networking management.

To show an example of how an application can be created with Rebol, we will create a simple task manager that allows users to create, modify, and delete tasks. The application will have a simple graphical interface that allows users to input new tasks, modify them, and delete them. We will also use an SQLite database to store user tasks.

Below is the code for the task management application in Rebol:

```rebol
REBOL []

; GUI layout definition of the application
view layout [
    title "Task Manager"
    across
    text "Task: "
    entry "Enter new task" new-task
```

```
    button "Add" [
        append tasks new-task/text
        save-tasks
        show-tasks
    ]
    button "Delete" [
        remove tasks edit-task/selected
        save-tasks
        show-tasks
    ]
    button "Exit" [quit]
    below
    text-list tasks data ["All tasks"]
]


; Function to save tasks in the SQLite database
```

```
save-tasks: does [
    sqlite-write %tasks.db tasks
]


; Function to load tasks from the SQLite database
load-tasks: does [
    tasks: sqlite-read %tasks.db
]


; Function to display tasks in the list
show-tasks: does [
    face/update
]


; Initialize tasks
tasks: []
```

```
; Start the application
load-tasks
show-tasks
```

In this code, we define a simple graphical interface for the task manager application using Rebol's layout. The graphical interface includes a text field for entering new tasks, buttons for adding and deleting tasks, as well as a list for displaying all tasks.

We also use the `save-tasks`, `load-tasks`, and `show-tasks` functions to save tasks in the SQLite database, load tasks from the database, and display tasks in the list, respectively.

Finally, we initialize the list of tasks with an empty array and start the application by loading tasks from the database and displaying them in the list.

Here is an example of code we could use to define the main functions of the application:

```rebol
; Define a map to store tasks
tasks: make object! [
    task-list: copy []

    ; Add a new task to the list
    add-task: func [name description deadline status] [
        new-task: make object! [
            name: name
            description: description
            deadline: deadline
            status: status
```

```
    ]
    append tasks.task-list new-task
]


; Display all tasks
display-tasks: func [] [
    foreach task tasks.task-list [
        print task.name
        print task.description
        print task.deadline
        print task.status
    ]
]


; Update the status of a task
update-status: func [name new-status] [
    foreach task tasks.task-list [
```

```
            if task.name = name [
                task.status: new-status
            ]
        ]
    ]


    ; Delete a task
    delete-task: func [name] [
        tasks.task-list: remove-each task [task.name = name]
    ]
]


; Use the defined functions to create and manage tasks
tasks.add-task "Go grocery shopping" "Buy milk, bread, and eggs" "2022-12-01" "in progress"
tasks.add-task "Prepare dinner" "Prepare a
```

```
special dinner for friends" "2022-11-25" "pending"

tasks.display-tasks

tasks.update-status "Go grocery shopping" "completed"

tasks.display-tasks

tasks.delete-task "Prepare dinner"

tasks.display-tasks
```

In this code example, we have defined a map to store tasks with an initial empty list. We then created four functions to add, display, update, and delete tasks. Using these functions, we created two new tasks, displayed all tasks, updated the status of one of the tasks, and finally deleted a specific task.

With its simple syntax and advanced features, Rebol is an excellent choice for quickly creating desktop, web, and embedded applications. We hope that this example has helped you better understand how to create an application with Rebol and has inspired you to further explore the capabilities of this language.

16. Glossary of basic technical terms for Rebol

List of the main technical terms used in Rebol programming:

1. ARGUMENT - Data passed to a function or program to be processed.

2. AS-IS - A reference to an object that is not modified during processing.

3. BLOCK! - An ordered collection of data, represented by square brackets [].

4. CAPTURE - Capturing output from a function or program for later use.

5. CONSTANT - An immutable value that cannot be changed once defined.

6. DATATYPE - The data type of a variable or object in Rebol, such as string, integer, block, etc.

7. FUNCTION - A block of code that performs a specific operation or task.

8. GET-WORD! - A type of value that represents a variable or function.

9. INHERITANCE - The concept of a class inheriting methods and properties from another class.

10. JOIN - Combining two or more values to create a new value.

11. KEY - A value associated with data in a map or dictionary.

12. LITERAL - A constant value that is not changed during processing.

13. MAP - A collection of data in key-value format.

14. NULL - A value representing the absence of data.

15. OBJECT - An instance of a class that contains data and methods.

16. PAREN! - A collection of data enclosed in parentheses ().

17. QUERY - Searching for data in a dataset.

18. REBOL - A dynamic and flexible

programming language.

19. SERIES - A sequence of data, such as a string or list.

20. THROW - Throwing an exception during program execution.

Glossary of technical terms in Rebol

Rebol is a versatile and powerful programming language that offers a wide range of features and possibilities. To fully leverage all its potential, it is essential to know and understand its key technical terms. In this glossary, you will find a complete list of all the major technical terms used in Rebol, along with a brief explanation of each.

1. Block: a block in Rebol is an ordered sequence of values and/or instructions

enclosed in square brackets []. Blocks can contain numbers, strings, lists, functions, and other blocks.

2. Function: a function in Rebol is a block of instructions that performs a specific operation or calculation. Functions can have input parameters and return an output value.

3. Return: the term "return" in Rebol refers to the value that a function returns when called. You can use the "return" statement to specify the return value of a function.

4. Object: an object in Rebol is a complex data structure that can contain attributes and methods. Objects allow you to organize and manipulate data efficiently.

5. Method: a method in Rebol is a function associated with an object that operates on it or its attributes. Methods can be called using the

"object/method" notation.

6. Word: a word in Rebol is an identifier that represents a variable, function, or another object within a program. Words can be used to assign values, define functions, and manipulate data.

7. Context: a context in Rebol is a set of variables and functions that are accessible from a certain point in the program. Contexts allow you to organize and structure code logically.

8. Model: a model in Rebol is a data structure that defines the shape and structure of an object. Models allow you to create complex and efficiently organized objects.

9. Iteration: iteration in Rebol refers to the process of repeating a block of instructions for a certain number of times or until a certain

condition is met. Iteration statements like "for" and "while" allow you to implement loops within a program.

10. Recursion: recursion in Rebol refers to the technique of defining a function that calls itself to solve a specific problem recursively. Recursion is useful for solving complex problems that can be divided into simpler subproblems.

11. Data: data in Rebol refers to the information or values that are processed or stored within a program. Data can be of different types, such as numbers, strings, lists, or objects.

12. Constant: a constant in Rebol is an immutable value that cannot be changed once assigned. Constants are used to define fixed values that should not be changed during program execution.

13. Expression: an expression in Rebol is a combination of values, operators, and functions that returns a result. Expressions can be used to calculate values, compare data, or perform mathematical operations.

14. Operator: an operator in Rebol is a symbol or word that specifies an operation to be performed on one or more values. Mathematical operators like +, -, *, / and logical operators like AND, OR, NOT are used to perform different operations on data.

15. Logic: logic in Rebol refers to the data type that represents the truth value of a proposition. Logical values can be True or False and are used to define conditions and checks within a program.

Indice

1. Introduction to Rebol pg.4

2. Rebol Installation pg.15

3. Syntax and coding rules in Rebol pg.20

4. Variables, data types, and basic operations in Rebol pg.29

5. Conditions and conditional statements in Rebol pg.34

6. Cycles and Iterations in Rebol pg.44

7.Definition and usage of Rebol functions pg.58

8.Parameters and Returns of Rebol Functions pg.67

9.Handling and throwing exceptions in Rebol pg.74

10.Debugging and testing of Rebol code pg.79

11.Creating User Interfaces with Rebol/View pg.85

12.Management of events and interactions in Rebol pg.91

13.File and Directory Manipulation with Rebol pg.98

14. Communicating with servers and external APIs in Rebol pg.104

15. Example of Application in Rebol pg.110

16. Glossary of basic technical terms for Rebol pg.120

www.ingramcontent.com/pod-product-compliance
Lightning Source LLC
Chambersburg PA
CBHW050305230526
45471CB00005B/2027